AMONG
WOODS
AND WATER

For the Northern Poetry Library,
edited by Lisa Matthews
and Melanie Ashby

NORTHERN
POETRY
LIBRARY

•

First published in 2016 by Literal Fish / Northern Poetry Library
ISBN: 978-0-9929514-2-9

Among Woods and Water is published as part of the Northern
Poetry Library project that includes the library-based poet
residencies featured in this anthology, along with a touring
exhibition, digital platform and spotlight activities across the North
East region. Both the book and the project are supported by Arts
Council England, Active Northumberland and other partners (see
Acknowledgements). The title draws upon the town of Morpeth's
motto 'Inter Sylvas et Flumina Habitans'. To find out more about
the project please visit the Northern Poetry Library website:
http://northernpoetrylibrary.org.uk

Book and cover by Lemony Design, lemonydesign.co.uk
Edited by Lisa Matthews, Lead Poet, and Melanie Ashby
Photography by Phyllis Christopher, with images also provided
by John Challis, Linda France and iStock by Getty
NPL branding by Founded, wearefounded.com
Printed in the UK by Field Print, on Cyclus Offset recycled paper

Among Woods and Water

An anthology of poetry
from Northumberland inspired by the
Northern Poetry Library

Contents

Northern Poetry Library

Counterculture troubadour of the 1960s Allen Ginsberg once said, "Poetry is the one place where people can speak their original human mind. It is the outlet for people to say in public what is known in private." Imagine then, the scope and power of a library dedicated solely to verse: all those poetic voices, all those experiences, all those perspectives on life – all freely available in a public space. In our fast-paced, monetized and information-drenched world, a poetry library is a rare and precious thing.

The Northern Poetry Library, established in the Sixties in Morpeth, Northumberland, is the largest collection of post-World War II poetry in England outside London. It is home to more than 15,000 volumes including a selection of anthologies, poetry books for children, and runs of journals and magazines. As a poetry library and archive it is unique, timeless and completely irreplaceable. Ginsberg – who travelled from the States to northeast England to read at hallowed poetry venue Morden Tower – would have loved diving into the collection.

Over its lifetime the library has seen many changes and it has grown from a small personal collection of poetry books into a significant civic and cultural asset. It has survived Morpeth's devastating flood waters of 2008 and today, like most libraries in the UK, continues to operate in challenging economic circumstances. In spite of hard times, however, this anthology is a celebration. The people in this book – among them practised and novice poets – who gathered in and around libraries across this region, from Berwick in the north, southwards to Alnwick, Morpeth, Hexham, Blyth and Newcastle, gave their energy to create something new. The book's title is drawn from the motto of NPL's hometown, Morpeth: 'Inter Sylvas et Flumina Habitans', which dates back to Norman times and translates as *living among woods and water*; we hope to confer to the library some of the motto's long and wild provenance.

The Northern Poetry Library did not appear fully realized and formed. Instead, and like poetry itself, it is a work-in-progress. The shelves tell a very human story, laying down in its collection a unique stratum of our times. The books held here are proof positive that all societies value poets and poetry. Because poetry, with its non-linear and unexpected forms, transcends traditional notions of narrative; the breathing space between the words – perhaps one of poetry's most unique features – is where we reside as readers, as communities and as a society.

Poetry doesn't speak for us, it is us. Feel your heart beating in your chest – that rhythm underpins the metre of poetic expression. The heartbeat of your birth mother was the first poetic expression you experienced and it lasted nine months or so, a never-ending surge of life that you can tap out on a table top. We naturally speak in a poetical form: for English speakers, iambic pentameter, cultivated as blank verse by Shakespeare, mimics the natural rhythms of speech. Poetry isn't, nor should it be, clever, obtuse or tricksy. For me it is everything that is human – determined by our physiology and by our interactions with our fellow creatures and environment. Every poem read or heard is, like each person, utterly unique. Our story is not one single story, it is many. Sylvia Plath in her poem Kindness wrote "The blood jet is poetry / There is no stopping it", and like the flood waters that pruned the NPL stock in 2008, there is no holding back the sheer power of poetics. Make no mistake, poetry is in you and that is why our library is such an important resource.

With a significant Arts Council (ACE) grant, together with generous contributions from a portfolio of partners and supporters, we have been able to contribute to the library's development in the second decade of the 21st Century. This book that you are holding right now, its content and all the current activity around NPL – the poets' residencies and commissions, the digital platform, spotlight activities, the anchored terset and touring exhibition – are ensuring that the collection lives long into the future. Along with the Scottish Poetry Library and the Poetry Library at Southbank Centre, the Northern Poetry Library forms a UK network of specialist library services.

Poetry doesn't speak for us, it is us. Feel your heart beating in your chest – that rhythm underpins the metre of poetic expression

The poet Rita Dove has said that "poetry is language at its most distilled and most powerful", and NPL is a storehouse of words so powerful it continues to defy the external forces that buffet it. Read this book, visit the collection (and/or the website), experience the range of voices and tell everyone about the Northern Poetry Library. Poetry is both the here-and-now and it is the future, and NPL continues to play a vital part in how poetry is created and disseminated. It has a unique Northern heritage to which this anthology contributes; it is also a globally relevant resource. It is a library we honour, celebrate and continue to develop. *There is no stopping it.*

Lisa Matthews, Lead Poet, Northern Poetry Library project

Berwick

...estinations

...Balboa saw,
...ut in the wind.
...s demons ride,
...h, tight by my side.

POETRY IN BERWICK

By poet-in-residence Degna Stone

It's been a wonderful experience browsing the shelves of
the Northern Poetry Library, choosing poems to share with
the groups. The poems sparked off wonderful, existential
conversations and inspired some truly beautiful poetry from the
groups I worked with.

The Berwick Library Group met during the winter months so
I wanted to shine a light on poems that could help us through
the dark nights – give us hope, make us laugh, tell us we're not
alone. The poets wrote in response to the prompt 'View from
a Window' and the poem Year Ending by Caroline Cook, which
describes a garden transformed by winter. This starting point
helped us to create work that felt very much about Berwick and
the borders and was firmly rooted in the season. Wallace Stevens'
poem Thirteen Ways of Looking at a Blackbird, with its numbered
tercets, provided inspiration for the title and form.

For the second group I focused on ekphrastic poetry as my
residency coincided with Middlesbrough Institute of Modern Art's
Where is the Line? exhibition at The Granary Gallery. We spent
the day at the gallery discussing poems like Vicki Feaver's The Red
Cupboard and Tim Turnbull's Ode on a Grayson Perry Urn, before
turning our attention to the artworks. We all fell in love with
Jenny Purrett's Storylines, drawn directly on the gallery walls and
featuring memories of Berwick handwritten on luggage labels.
Purrett's work introduced us to the idea of 'primal landscapes',
the sense that you take the place you grew up with you wherever
you go. Within that theme are ideas of place, of belonging, of
borders. Perfect for Berwick...

Hold Fast to Dreams

If you have children give them magic —
conjure the scene without inducing fright,
because whatever the news, you are still alive.

Why are we leaving in such unreadiness,
our hands unwrapping the darkness,
binding black hostilities?

They draw on their last cigarettes
just at the moment of their vanishing,
carried in the cold night
where light-enthralling silence lies.

I see, then, that a kind of faith prevails —
truth needs no eloquence.
Nothing is random, nothing goes to waste,
          you're human.

Degna Stone

Cento [n] – a poem made up of lines from existing poems:
Dreams (Langston Hughes) • Advice for My Daughters (Julia Darling)
• Ode on a Grayson Perry Urn (Tim Turnbull) • How to Deal with Terrible
News (Julia Darling) • Seven Questions About the Journey (Don Paterson) •
December (Carol Ann Duffy) • It Looks So Simple from a Distance... (Anne
Stevenson) • Truce (Paul Muldoon) • Our Lady of the Sorrows (Pippa Little)
• Christmas Sparrow (Billy Collins) • Winterbourne (Jacob Polley) • For a
Five-Year-Old (Fleur Adcock) • Silence (Mourid Barghouti) • Courtyards in
Delft (Derek Mahon) • Human Beings (Adrian Mitchell)

"Everyone, regardless of where they grew up, has a 'primal landscape'."

Genius Loci

*"Everyone, regardless of where they grew up,
has a 'primal landscape'."*

I see you sitting on that roadside bank
level with the tall, brittle, yellow grass
as it bends and then it breaks in wind unheard from the road,
reaching for a low, brown hill under damp, coastal clouds.

    Inside Peckham flats a blanket drapes,
    green and orange and indigo.
    A wheel spins the day into life
    and a thousand colours burst
    onto a grey concrete exterior.

Down days, when cold grates lay ashen,
chilled the fingers and toes of life,
home was a frozen, primal landscape.
Up days were those warmed with a blaze.

    Show me the ocean that Balboa saw,
    set me to sail white, taut in the wind.
    Give me a horse swift as demons ride,
    then set you, *ich bitte dich*, tight by my side.

Ancient stone: a windswept child's playground.
Lines of green and yellow, rain-stained walls
anchored between shifting sea and sky.
Racing wheels, racing clouds;
        remembered laughter.

    If I am lost, found crying in the maze,
    don't lead me home, point me a different tack
    and when the sunrise gilds another day
    I'll take my chance, go dance that newfound way.

Participants from Where is the Line? workshop

*Tricia Coxon, Anna Edgar, Rebecca Harris,
Bryan Langley and Philomena Ulyatt.*

13 Ways of Looking from a Window

I.

Heavy rain spatters on a plain and grubby pane.
Here is a grey, subdued Northern Matisse,
no Prince Charming to wake it from neglected slumber.

II.

I peer out of the kitchen window to Branxton Hill,
caught in a spider's web of high telephone wires,
weeping for bloody Flodden's carnage.

III.

Thin willow withies whip the hostile sky
and yellow rosebuds taunt the thorn-scratched wind.
The giant pines are dancing to the beat.

IV.

No sleep for me as the days break ever earlier.
Pigeons and rooks set up home in multi-storey branches.
They squabble from first light, and the seagulls screech back.

V.

Like winter's moon, silent and pale,
a barn owl lilting over the shadowy field,
it came, silent and pale over the low stone wall.

VI.

Brightness of the sky tells the time.
Sparrows coming and going do not interest the child.
Far away – horizon where sea meets sky.

VII.

In this view is a huge and glorious sycamore.
Today, in wind and wet, its bare branches poke
their black fingers across, prodding and accusing.

VIII.

Sparrows bustle
whilst windy gusts conspire to hinder them in their task.
A splay of small white feathers – only sign of sparrowhawk's call.

IX.

The dreich garden and frozen birdbath join the wake –
migrant starlings, expecting their de-lousing bath, slide and skate.
Graceless, they clatter into each other shaken and bemused.

X.

The colours, clouded by the pulsing rain,
are doused until the greys alone remain.
Then deepest red electrifies the scene.

XI.

The sudden lighting of two acid orange streetlamps
illuminates a stage set through my uncurtained window,
as the winter afternoon closes in around me.

XII.

An unseen toddler asks: "Why do gardens have fences?"
"To keep the cats and dogs out and you safe," border logic replies.
I think of cats, dogs, weeds and people, of Flodden Field.

XIII.

Raucous and raw as a winter dawn trailing scarves
tattered and grey, rumpled and red.
One curved white feather twirling down.

Berwick Library Poetry Group

*Anna Edgar, Colin Fleetwood, Bryan Langley,
Barbara Prater and Philomena Ulyatt.*

Alnwick

POETRY IN ALNWICK
By poet-in-residence Carolyn Jess-Cooke

I worked with two groups in Alnwick between November 2015 and January 2016. My group of Year 9 pupils at Duchess Community High School in Alnwick came to poetry with a huge amount of curiosity and energy, and a desire to understand *what poetry can do*. We built houses filled with poetry, 3D paper artworks inscribed with our thoughts about home and belonging; we wrote poems about fear and hope; we wrote group poems that played with rhythm and repetition, and used our imagination to fill the spaces between lines. By the end of the residency, the pupils had engaged with numerous works from the Northern Poetry Library and explored the possibilities of language and music.

My group of adult writers met at the Bailiffgate Museum weekly and developed new poetry whilst engaging with poets housed at the NPL. It was a wonderful experience to 'workshop' each other's work-in-progress, giving feedback on what was strong about the poem, and thinking carefully about how a poem could be rendered even more effective – essentially, coming 'off' the page and forging a lens through which we could see life anew.

The residency changed everyone who participated, including the poet-in-residence. The schoolchildren presented me with a beautiful orchid plant (that miraculously continues to flower) and a card indicating their enjoyment of the workshops. The Bailiffgate writers commented on the 'empowering and supportive atmosphere' of the sessions; the group hopes to continue the workshop themselves in the long term.

The House of Rest

A History of Josephine Butler, feminist and social reformer,
born Corbridge, Northumberland, 1828

George and I have found a second house
to rent at two-hundred-and-fifty pounds a year –
for this we shall provide a home for thirteen women.
I wish it could accommodate more, but for now
we shall make a little heaven
for those stained and dying Magdalenes to live
in comfort, to come to know their God
before they meet Him.
                              Their time is short, despite
our doctor offering his services pro bono. He can but
bring relief of pain as they bear out their day. Remarkable
that Eliza, the youngest, counts herself fortunate
to die in such a place! So many others have to take men
even while they're dying, she says. How it must harrow them
to die with such indignity!
                              Her words
have drilled through me all the day long. Our House
of Incurables puts us all at great risk of harm by those
who consider us to be furthering the cause
of prostitution (perish the thought!). I have been
spat at, called a villain and a whore, and yet
my mind will not be turned: I must do more.

Carolyn Jess-Cooke

What is Hope?

Hope is the ringing bells of freedom.
Hope is when people come together to help one another.
Hope is unity in the kingdom,
When mankind treats another like a brother.

Hope is having someone to rely on.
Hope is when you finally hit the crossbar.
Hope is when you connect with a song.
Hope is when you get an A star.

Year 9 poetry group at Duchess Community High School •
Emily Barrett, Erin Bell, Emily Curry, Ruairi Fletcher, Josh France,
Olivia Gerrard, Courtney Ingleton, James P Keane, Connor Richardson,
Andrew Surtees and Palesa Thompson.

Sway

I

An Autumn Play

A surprising riverscape is revealed
As the greenest scenes of summer wane.
The stage has altered.
Now it is earthy browns, mottled leaves.
I thought it was the start of decay.
But the foliage curtain has raised
To unveil
Quite a different set.
A willow tree.
Horizontal, arms and fingers dip
Into the listening river
While her mossy roots reach up.
A frilly petticoat of fungi and lichen
Drips prettily around her ankles.
Along her trunk life teams
Can you hear?
And offshoots spiral skywards.
These small thin branches point towards the sun.
Clouds of tiny leaves
Halo their heads.
It's not a rehearsal, this
Germination
In the midst of decay.

II
Fading Away

Rendezvous Café down on the front.
Cups of tea warm winter fingers –
white from wandering streets on teenage feet.
Waiting to be noticed by passing boys
who laugh at me, my spotty face,
my fat body, slowly changing,
getting thinner, every day.

Nil by mouth, self prescribed.
Starved of sugar, acne fades.
One day, someone will say
haven't you got nice skin –
watch you don't fall
down that pavement crack.

III
Tenderness

Don't despair
When the wind blows cold and constant from the north
And icy tears streak your ashen face below a woolly hat
It is winter after all, and you know it will soon end.
Don't despair
When persistent rain drowns all hope
And dampens the little pleasures
A winter's day can bring –

Remember spring
Coiled just around the corner
Waiting to surprise you again
Like an unexpected cup of tea in bed.
It says come in, take off your coat,
Be welcome
Life is stirring in the fields
and hedgerows.

IV
A Space Punctuated by Trees

A feather alights on a leaf
Quills of sunlight inscribe the forest
Illuminated branches wait in quiet hope
Under a shawl of moss and fungus worms burrow
Ingrained in this silent arbour
Nature waits
For the bloom of bluebells
For the birds

V
Time on the Line

I marvel at the carefully-crafted, tiny-waisted skirt I had sewn
                                                    for my daughter.
White embroidery anglaise dotted with little strawberries,
it catches the sunlight as I peg it on the washing line.

Here, my small son's pop-buttoned trousers with an
appliquéd bib,
next, a pretty cream-coloured pageboy's outfit with frilly cuffs
borne bravely by his brother.

Some dolls' clothes – a little, lacy, green knitted dress
worn by Natalie, a favourite doll,
won in a 'Guess the Name' competition.

I am pegging out my memories on this line.

Tears well up as my heart lurches backwards
to those mothering days long gone
when I could enfold my three chicks in one embrace.
My life is full and happy, I know,
but for a moment, I am knocked off balance
by time blowing in the wind.

VI
January

A filigree of rowan branches shivers
lit by a lamp's reflection

through half-closed shutters.
Headstrong, you push into a squall

bend downhill towards the fire blazing
in the Blue Waiting Room. The wind scours

your skin, tosses autumn rags
into the gutter, ruffles

the surface of puddles. Blows
your umbrella inside out –

Silver spikes frame an unexpected view.

When you return, the rowan tree still stands,
curls roots into the earth, bare branches in the storm.

Winter light pours honey down the terrace.

Group at the Bailiffgate Museum ·
Mary Atkinson, Romaine Barclay-Kim, Mags Bell, Pamela Gormally,
Katie Scott and Philip Stuckey.

Blyth, and
Newcastle University

POETRY IN BLYTH AND AT NEWCASTLE UNIVERSITY

By poet-in-residence John Challis

As Michael Donaghy said, "good poetry is thoroughly unpredictable." What it is and how it should be written is constantly surprising. In following a set of rules we do not necessarily produce great poetry. The workshops in Blyth tackled this conundrum and exposed the participants to as many poets and types of poem as possible (from lyrical to experimental), giving them a crash course in contemporary poetry. It was an immense pleasure to see the group grow in confidence over the weeks, and to see their poems take new and exciting routes. Inspired by Blyth's working history as a port town, we looked at many poems about working lives. The collaborative poem here focuses on Blyth's industry and people, and actively archives the memories of the town in all its "washed-up glory".

The second half of my residency took place at Newcastle University where I worked with three distinct and diverse groups: Ageing Creatively, Medicine in Literature and the Arts at Newcastle, and GemArts. With the help of Newcastle Centre for the Literary Arts and the Robinson Library, the sessions took place in the coveted Bloodaxe Archive, where we were given access to the manuscripts and letters of some of the world's leading poets, published by Bloodaxe Books. By considering what an archive is and responding to its contents, each group produced a unique collaborative poem that explored what the concept of an archive means to them. You could say that a poem is like an archive, a repository for memories, thoughts and ideas. The jointly-written poem presented here reflects the wide and diverse interests and lives of the poets who wrote it.

The Learner

Stuck behind a learner when the limit increases
I remember what it's like to master the instruments,
clutch, gearstick, indicator, wipers, mirrors, lights,

as everyone around you passes expressionless
like the frames of half-built cars shifting down the line
while mechanical limbs twitch missing pieces in.

My arm on the window, at this age it comes easily,
this marriage with machine, brakes know when to slow,
acceleration mans itself when there's road to drive.

At the roundabout where land opens like a centrefold
that Tynemouth lighthouse searches,
I wait a chevron back for the learner to decide,

the radio full of useless tunes, and watch as the field
becomes conscious with geese taking flight.

John Challis

Tides

I

Eight hundred years ago till now, our town has grown.
First salt, then ships and coal and industries well known.
A river flowing out to sea, a pier on either side.
A sandy beach around the bay washed by incoming tide.

The beach is where I love to be in rain, wind, snow or sun,
golden sand, a prom, the dunes, something for everyone.
A play park for the children, the Battery museum to see.
Try a delicious ice cream, take fish and chips home for tea.

II

Drifting past the memories,
transitions in a dream.
Past the sleepy harbour,
past the soaking green.
Man-made giants stand in the distance
as if to wave goodbye.
No matter where I roam,
you're still home. You're still home.

III

The seat belt signs illuminate
as we start our last descent,
then banking down across the dark
North Sea, I start to feel content.

The flaps and engines move and roar,
and we touch down safe and sound.
Pick up luggage; through customs pass,
to the taxi stand I bound.

On country lanes, through towns and villages,
these pass along the way.
Speeding to the place I love,
for too long I have been away.

I see the sea, wind turbines grand;
the view fills me with joy,
then into the town that I've called
my home ever since I was a boy.

IV

Here, in this square set aside for cars, where shoppers
ply carts brimmed with provisions, or wait, laden, for taxis,

trains once brought thousands, third-class and hungry,
from every dispossessed, squire-haunted hamlet

to a century of new bearings: to slipways, deep mines,
a river of coal; to fevers, bitter winds, sudden falls of stone.

Here, in this same space, where once, as a curiosity,
a great whale was displayed in all its grey, washed-up glory.

V

Coal dust lingers in the air. We left on the ebbing tide
passing Bolckow Breakers Yard and Blyth Shipbuilders.
Cranes stand like forgotten dragons. Bate's pithead
wheels are still and rusted. West, North and South staithes;
stark timbers reaching to the sky. Men with chainsaws
work like beavers, cutting them down for matchsticks.
Silent testimonies to lost industries. We sail between
the pierheads to meet the deep rolling sea. We hear
the low mournful wail of North Blyth's foghorn,
as the town's lights fade into deepening night.

Blyth Library Poetry Workshops •
Robert Cessford, Paul Crate, Eileen Darling,
George B Peacock and Sam Tuff.

Archives

I. Final Archive

And what is the collective noun
for a stack of diaries?
The first, a small red volume
is zipped on three sides.

Scarlet card wraps treasured pages.
Four children camping, fishing, fighting,
shared the nightly chore of writing.
Fifty years ago; now a holiday relived.

My evanescent track of life is nailed
at intersections by events in the greater world.
Where was I when Kennedy was shot?
When Neil Armstrong landed on the moon?

Beneath the bench amongst strips of wood
that might come in handy when the going is good,
lie bottles of wine, red elder and flower
slowly maturing for another year.

I hear the rusty hinge of my grey box complain
as white-gloved hand disturbs once precious bits of lives;
without them, and this tiny ancient coffin,
picked-over, pale, the memory bones alone remain.

On ice white slab,
rounded, mounded, shrouded form,
formaldehyde scents the non alive
–   The final archive?

II. Incognito

Let me clasp you in my folded arms
and whisper to you a message:

blood clots dissolved in old jars of rat poison,
grey pairs of TED stockings stuffed in a drawer,

unfinished notebooks, associations and connections
linking the public and professional with the private –

jump out of my history of searches,
the time I discovered incognito

those indigestible secrets
stuck fast in my craw –

bright words gone tumbling into fog,
a captured thought escaping in the mist.

Stop, breathe; hear children's laughter and silent tears
drifting together through the spiral of life.

III. Veil and Cloak

'Happenings' I shine a light on. Some I veil
and cloak but they are like burning embers
in a deep, dark recess. Shall I venture into this cave?

Closeted behind long dresses,
an empty box lies in a safe,
'Top Secret' marked on the sides.

Treasured within the fortress of my heart,
memories paint shades of black, yellow and red.
Sorrow and joy have settled here, made my heart their home.

Newcastle University Group Writers:

Ageing Creatively •
Richard Day, Janet Devoy, Ali Finlayson, Janet Grieve,
Mary Learoyd and Heather Wilson.

Medicine in Literature and the Arts at Newcastle •
Rosie Anderson, Annie Harrison, Eleanor Holmes, Vikki Park,
Pauline Pearson, Salma Sopian and Sue Spencer.

GemArts •
Shazya Aslam, Iftekhar Khan and Ruth Nyimba.

Morpeth

POETRY IN MORPETH

By poet-in-residence Jo Colley

My residency explored the power of poetry to live in the mind and affect people's lives from childhood onwards. I worked with three different groups in Morpeth: an elderly group of residents from the Riverside Care Home, a group of students from King Edward VI School, and the ViP (Visually Impaired) Bookgroup.

My approach, called Missing Lines, was inspired by my late mother's ability to remember lines of poetry. She lived until she was 91, and even in her last weeks quoted lines of poetry in her conversations. Often, she was not sure where they came from, but they remained in her mind, and she enjoyed the sound and feel of them in her mouth. "They told me, Heraclitus, they told me you were dead," she might say....

I wanted to know if other elderly people had similar 'missing lines', how they had learned them as children, if they ever thought about poetry now. I started in the Riverside Care Home and found a wealth of lines to kickstart the project. After researching a poem's origin, I took the complete piece back to the residents for choral reading and discussion.

As a next step, I shared these lost lines with younger writers, part of a creative writing group at King Edward VI. With the facilitation of teacher Rachel Camsell, the lost lines were offered to the students as gifts to begin new work, prompted by the words of poets of the past. In this poetry relay between generations, the old poems are heard again, then taken in directions unforeseen by their originators.

The project has also led me to the ViP group, meeting in Morpeth library once a month. Amid a discussion of the importance of sound and rhythm, more lost lines were unearthed... *Softly along the road of evening*. The group's interest in contemporary poetry has been stirred by their act of collective remembering, with subsequent sessions on Wendy Cope and Gillian Clarke. Their responses exposed the ability of poetry to stir memories, to evoke powerful emotions, to delight and entertain.

Cold Grey Sea

Prompted by Alfred Lord Tennyson's Break, Break, Break

We looked for seaglass on a beach I did not know
in light I could not recognise. My heart revolved
inside my ribs, a cold carcase on a butcher's hook.

Eyes down, I cased the pebbles, while you
kept silent, your switchblade tongue
slid back inside your mouth.

Alone together, we detectorised the stones,
gathered what we could: aquamarine tears,
opaque crumbs, mere fragments. Not enough

to penetrate this complicated fog. I took off
my shoes, immersed my feet in the north sea.
The waves tried to breach the wall my head

was making, to undo with water what was built
with words. How I would that my tongue could utter
the thoughts that arise in me.

Jo Colley

Riverside Villanelle

The place where everybody calls us pet,
where history lingers flowing like a stream.
We all still live here: haven't vanished yet.

I wonder if my life has been a dream,
as memories mingle, slip and disagree.
The place where everybody calls us pet.

Look at us now: we are not what we seem.
Behind these masks are things you cannot see:
we all still live here: haven't vanished yet.

Although you might think we have drunk the cream,
we choose to be instead of not to be.
The place where everybody calls us pet.

We're staying here until we float downstream.
To later living well, we have the key.
We all still live here: haven't vanished yet.

Until we're wanted in the sunbeam team,
returning rivers to the mother sea.
The place where everybody calls us pet.
We all still live here: haven't vanished yet.

*Adapted from conversations with residents at the
Riverside Care Home, with special thanks to Celia,
Marguerite and Michael.*

I Remember, I Remember

By Olivia Sheed, after Thomas Hood's poem of the same name

I remember, I remember
A bitter night in December
Where a wolf called out to the night

His howls lost to the wind
Which did cry and sing
To cover and hide my fright

The tree trunks became twisted
As I hid and listed
The scars he would leave on my skin

He pounced on my body
Grabbed me while sobbing
And whispered I belonged to him

The Traveller

By Tom Berry, after The Listeners by Walter de la Mare

"Is there anybody there?" said the traveller.
The traveller stood still, wind flapping his coat,
his boots caked with mud, twigs, grass.
No-one replied.

He shouted again,

his voice hoarse and dry.
His beard seemed to quiver at the sound.
No-one replied.

He shouted again.
His backpack held the items for his journey:
with hunched back he carried it, but with pride
he bore it.
No-one replied.

He did not shout again.
He heard the tiny beeps, becoming slower, rarer.
Then they stopped. The man's journey was over.
The only reply was crying.

Shadow Figure

By John Heywood, after My Shadow by RL Stevenson

Shadow Figure glides down the street.
Hovers below the lamppost.
The dark light flickers,
Once, Twice, Thrice.

Shadow Figure,
Shadow Figure.
Who are you?
Why are you here?
Where did you come from?
And, and, and...
I don't know.
No-one knows.

Except Shadow Figure.

Watching, Waiting.
What will Shadow Figure do?
Watching, Waiting.
Cloaked in blackness.
Lifeless legs. Cold ground.
Shadow Figure's worth it.

Skins of ourselves, empty shells.
Our silhouettes.
Our silhouettes.
In the day, inhabited.
In the night, uninhabited.

Shadow Figure floats along the street.
Lingers below the lamppost.
The dark light flickers.
Once, Twice, Thrice.

•

POEM INSPIRED BY CONVERSATIONS WITH THE
VIP (VISUALLY IMPAIRED) BOOKGROUP

They Told Us...

They told us, when we read at night, weak torchlight
glowing underneath the sheets: your eyes will wear out.
Back then, enclosed inside the story, we'd risk anything
to reach the finish line, could not rest until the closure
of an ending, happy or sad.

We looked for answers in the printed word, preferred
the black and white of text to hillside, seaside, cityscape.
Our imaginations stirred, made stages for the worlds
created by those who spun a tale, or rhymed a rhyme,
or made us laugh.

Escapist, maybe. But there were situations we needed
to escape: unhappiness, or tedium, bullying or worse.
What we learned allowed us to prepare. Confined
in our provincial towns, we wanted more. Our eyes
were opened there, along the dusty shelves

and they will never close.

*With thanks to Ros Markham, librarian for reader development in
Ponteland Library, and members of the ViP group. Below is a poem
by group member Ace Oldroyd, inspired by lines from Storm in the
Black Forest by DH Lawrence: "Jugfull after jugfull of pure white liquid
fire / Bright white, / Tipples over and spills down / And is gone."*

Cream Jugs

The table, dressed for a country tea, heaved with all things good,
waiting sturdily for the crowd which soon would swoop keenly
                                        on its bounty.
The scene was set; smooth linen cloths woven fine as silk,
Heavy jugs, squat, round, reliable shapes with sensible handles
                                        and large-lipped spouts,
Sit smugly on the table like Cheshire Cats,
All dressed in summer colours of blue-washed glaze and
                                        strawberry trellis.

Bowls to match in shallow shape and edged with yellow.

Large, lush strawberries sit smugly in the bowls,
Basking in their own loveliness,
Sensual shapes of red, round fruit
Lazily anticipating their crowning glory of white.
Scones, pale-coloured, sit upright on their plates,
Smart and neat, fluted shapes of golden goodness,
And rich, proper yellow butter, melting in the sun.

Jugfull after jugfull of pure white liquid cream,
Bright cream,
Tipples over and spills down
Into the waiting fruit,
Drenching the red in purity
Until the luscious berries are lost in bright white liquid heaven,
Cool and clean, pouring in smooth, embracing stream
Until the berries drown in pooling pure white cream.

After the feast, each jug sits empty, its summer bounty poured
and drained into the sweetest fruit.
The cream, clean, sweet and smooth,
Loved by those that took its riches,
Leaves a white rim in each painted jug,
To be washed and rinsed and clean until once again
Filled with nature's liquid purity.

Jugfull after jugfull of pure white liquid cream,
Bright cream,
Tipples over and spills down
Into the gorgeous fruit,
And is gone.

Hexham

POETRY IN HEXHAM

By poet-in-residence Linda France

Inspired by Transition Tynedale's Edible Hexham initiative – small patches of ground and sundry containers turned over to growing vegetables, fruit and herbs across the town – I knew I wanted my residency to be about the poetry of food. On the heels of my writing about gardens and flowers, it seemed a natural next step to explore the poetic potential of what we cultivate to put on our plates. Gathering our 'luggage-label and tree renga' on Apple Pressing Day at Hexham Farmer's Market was an auspicious beginning to a project that turned out even more fruitful than I'd hoped.

A small group met for regular workshops in Hexham Library. We warmed ourselves round the hearth of poems by Pablo Neruda, Vicki Feaver, Joy Harjo, David Harsent among others, celebrating the pleasures of cooking and eating – a perfect antidote to stormy winter evenings. The poems we read sparked some of our own, culminating in a small pot-luck banquet laid out on one of the library tables – source for our lip-smacking collaborative poem, Mezze in Midwinter.

More guerilla tactics were used to introduce poetry to Transition Tynedale's larger group and the AGM saw everyone sharing thoughts about what poetry and food meant to them. A satellite session arose from an invitation to work with the University of the Third Age (U3A), turning the residency full circle as apples popped up on the menu again. The Northern Poetry Library was the perfect muse for a residency brimming with creativity and abundance. Here is just a small taste of its nourishing yield.

Bottle

Every mealtime it graced our table
like a candlestick or a vintage wine,

with the salt and pepper, the bowl
of sugar, speckled with amber tea-stains –

our kitchen altar, where we'd gather
round a square of scratched Formica.

In a house without books, it was here
I learnt to read, sounding out the letters,

HP, ™, counting 9 o'clock on Big Ben –
red and blue rubric of the lion who married

a unicorn (my fiery Dad? my sweet Mam?)
by appointment to HM the Queen.

The knowledge of its dark vinegary tang
I sensed was a father's preserve.

Hungry, I read everything I could get
my hands on, whippersnapper legs

stinging, slapped for asking too many
questions the teacher said was sauce.

Linda France

52 Ways of Looking at Apples

Yellow apples
green apples
red apples

picking washing crushing
everyone loves our juice!

I'm five
in a Devon woodland
find old apple trees

the whole street's tree
to harvest for cooking

war-time – queuing
for her favourites
Egremont Russets

a washing-up bowl
Halloween bobbing

climbing the apple tree
when my legs
weren't really long enough

Golden Delicious
not so delicious any more

an apple ladder
in Jim's orchard
wasps, red admiral and me

pick – pause – admire
dig in – crunch – enjoy

standing on my pony's back
to reach crisp pale fruit
Wykin Pippins

I prefer
pears!

weekend – friends and freedom
apple picking and pressing
to remember forever

us apple-bashers
Lewis, our quality controller

Gascoyne Scarlet   Ashmead's Kernel
Beauty of Bath   Bloody Ploughman   Slovakia, age nine
Keswick Codlin   Greensleeves   drunk on fermented juice

boxes stacked
up to the eaves   falling and falling
apple scent in stone   caught by Newton

three trees – one gives up
one's begrudging   *Howgate Wonder* –
the third's a thug, heavy-laden   one apple per pie

every time I eat an apple
the memory   forgotten homemade cider –
of my parent's orchard   Lewisham Calvados

all the apples eaten by mice
except those wrapped   our whole kitchen
in the Church Times   coated with smashed apples

a glut of crimson
climbing knobbly branches   the Kentish farmer, yes,
crabapple jelly   his Worcester *Permains*

orchard-sleeper
ancient ramshackle one –   mmmmmm
his are the apples we buy   delicious

under the apple tree
Thy Mother bare thee in love
with joy and full of grace

apples tied to the clothes line
for birthday party games

a dearth
until Dad's death
then one lone *Bramley*

trying to recreate
their Dutch apple attic

scrumping – the risk
more delicious
than the apples we nicked

breakfast every day
from that Durham tree

harvest calling
young man in an orchard
everything falls

twenty years in America
I never tasted a good apple

Bonfire Night
scrambling up
Granfer's gnarly apple tree

Norfolk Beauty
you are the apple of my eye

apple-ducking
in an abandoned tin bath
all soaking wet

homemade spider cider –
scrumptious!

at Billy Bell's
we're making pies
with *Arthur Turner*

climbing her first tree
plucking her first apple

I hide
apple cores
everywhere

                    my grandparent's orchard –
                       the smell of happiness

back in Himachal Pradesh
we compare pink cheeks
to our northern apples

        "the silver apples of the moon
        the golden apples of the sun"

in Nana's garden
running slap-bang
into her apple tree

           from picking to pressing
           to drinking – perfection

Claygate Pearmain   Laxton's Superb
James Grieve   Scotch Bridget
Ellison's Orange   Sunset

         we loved our mother's pies
         joked about the skins left in

O golden globes
O russet cheeks
O Eve

                  unimaginable –
          a world without apples.

An Apple Day Renga,
gathered at Hexham Farmer's Market,
Northumberland,
on 10th October 2015.

Apple Day Renga •

Anon (x 6)
Birtley Aris
Jean Aris
Jo Aris
John Askew
Kat Auld
Catherine Barraclough
Elizabeth Beardsley
Mark Benjamin
Matilda Bevan
Wendy B
Robert Bluck
Tanya Chanidel
Andrew Corder
Sarah Dunn
Ellen & Jessie
Khaled Elsamman
Linda France
Anabel Gammidge
Jackie Gaughan
Bridget Hewitt
Alison Hewson
Bill Jefferson
Elizabeth Leonard
Margaret Lewis
Peter Lewis
Lucas Majer
Jane Michie (and Lucy)

Ros Normandale
Gillian Orrell
Mary Oswell
Bronwyn Payne
Lewis Payne
Megan Payne
Ron Peacher
Debbie Reed
Mary Richard
Magnus Riddel
Andrew Sandann
Peter Samsom
James Sawbey
William Sparksman
Sue Seymour
Michael Turner-Cox
Margot Waters
Julia Whitaker

Mezze in Midwinter •

Birtley Aris
Jo Aris
Matilda Bevan
Linda France
Patricia Gillespie
Rosie Hudson
Rosalind Normandale
Simone Silver Path

Mezze in Midwinter

And start with salt, oil –
beginner of dinners –
olives from a hot hillside.

And alchemy of cheese,
butter, flour transformed
by steamy intensities.

And remember Brillat-Savarin –
"truffles are the diamond of the kitchen",
emerging black and sparkling from leaf mould.

And a spoonful tastes of the past,
of water and summer and hedgerows
and cauldrons and gold.

And Bramley's undressed, she's lost
her glossy green gown
and plays camouflage.

And our mouths are full of Africa –
lions, savannah,
the sun inside her.

And so we dance on the altar
of our lives, casting veils
from rounded bellies – attar of roses.

Hexham Library,
30th November 2015.

Northern Poetry Library
in Morpeth

POETRY AT THE NORTHERN POETRY LIBRARY

By poet-in-residence Lisa Matthews

As Lead Poet, over the summer of 2015 I made the library a workday home and got the chance to take my time among the books, diving into the stock as well as interacting with staff and users. Spending time in NPL took me back to my own days as a Library Assistant and it was an honour to be part of the fixtures and fittings. I loved seeing the staff in action, working with queries and guiding people to books, eager to share their knowledge and passions, and open to learning more about the collection. The NPL is a special collection embedded in the public library and for many people – including library staff – the run of poetry books can seem a bit esoteric and hard to access. Some of my aim in working with the staff as a group has been to let them see behind the scenes of poetry from a writer and poetry-lover's perspective.

For this anthology I led a small-scale workshop on pieces about poetry and libraries. What emerged is a collaboration with Julie Brown, a poet herself and one of the staff involved with NPL enquiries. As the library's continued development is an ongoing story so I feel it is fitting to present this as a work-in-progress while attempting to shed light on the process of creating a poem, with a description of the writing workshop. I also present my notes on a new poetic form – the anchored terset – I created for the library, given life to by the staff during my summer residency.

I want to thank Julie, Chris, Paul, Pat and Shirley, and all the NPL and Active Northumberland staff for their support and insight. Walking into someone's workplace is always a challenge; the welcome I received and the way all the staff embraced this project is testimony to how much they value the service they provide.

Villanelle for the Library

among woods and water
between words and meaning
a story prepares to be heard

in the telling, voices wait
birds fall below quiet clouds
among woods and water

solitary hart, black butterfly
all is all and everything is alone
a story prepares to be heard

be brave my sister, be still
there are many miles to go
among woods and water

when the sun falls below the
horizon, and something calls home
a story prepares to be heard

we both leave our mark, press
our hands on these relocated walls
among woods and water
a story prepares to be heard

Lisa Matthews

BLUEPRINT: A COLLABORATION

This workshop activity requires at least two people, one of whom is a facilitator. When doing this exercise with a group, it helps to arrange the room so as to sit in a round.

1. Each person writes a single paragraph about a particular subject – in this case we wrote about poetry. Write for ten minutes maximum, trying not to pause or edit.

2. The facilitator then guides participants through a series of editorial steps, of which the following are examples, to be carried out and marked up on their paragraph. It can help to use different colours for the various steps. Underline:
- *the final six words of your paragraph*
- *the image you like most*
- *a single word in the text selected at random*
- *all the verbs or adjectives*
- *the middle line of the paragraph*
- *another random word plus the two words before and after it*
- *the opening eight words of your paragraph*

3. Put the paragraphs to one side and do something else for at least twenty minutes – another writing activity or a take break.

4. Coming together as a group, each person starts a new piece of paper, preferably lined. Led by the facilitator, each writes the first of the 'underlinings' of their paragraph on the new sheet – in this case the final six words of the paragraph – on the top line. The paper is then passed to the person on the left.

5. Beginning a new line under the first, each participant writes

the next underlining from their paragraph – in this case their favourite image. Continue with this process of writing a new line harvested from each person's own paragraph, passing the paper on, like a game of consequences.

6. Sometimes the facilitator may choose to do particular things with the underlinings – for instance, requiring one of the words to be repeated.

7. Once all the steps have been carried out, one line following another in the round to create a full-grown 'poem', participants then review what appears on their piece of paper. Use the material as a draft to create a new poem or piece of prose.

What follows is one of the poems Julie Brown and I created using this collaborative method. The original as it appeared on the sheet of paper is shown below, followed by Julie's progressive edit and then mine, as together we refine the piece into a poem. We made an effort not to change too many of the words from the original. This is a work-in-progress and shows just one of the ways people can work jointly on poems in writing workshop settings.

ORIGINAL WRITING

Poetry Is A Blueprint Of Emotion
Come forth boldly without fear
Between between between
To be dipped into
A hidden door in a library wall
Left unsaid allowing the self
Our lives that make it

Poetry is a Blueprint of Emotion

Come forth boldly without fear to read
Between between between the inky lines
To be dipped into perhaps to find
A hidden door in a library wall, where words
Left unsaid allow the self to touch
Our lives that make it indelible.

Blueprint

Come forth boldly without fear to read
Between, between, between the inky lines
To be dipped into, perhaps to find

A hidden door in a library wall, where words
Left unsaid allow the self to touch
The lives that make it indelible.

THE ANCHORED TERSET

The anchored terset (sic) is a new poetry form created during my residency at the Northern Poetry Library. It is a four-line, three-word poem – the first three lines consist of one word each, the final line a full stop. On one level it's a bit of fun intended to generate interest in the library and in contemporary poetry. However, I was also deadly serious about wanting to create something with genuine literary provenance. A 'tercet' is a three-line unit of poetry and my spelling with its 's' is a phonetic reference to traditional tercets while also being a nod to another word with poetic resonance: 'terse'. This new terset puts jazz hands on its brevity, *look at me* it says, with its ostentatious (mis)spelling.

HOW SHORT?

The poetic form haiku distills a poem to just three lines: in its traditional Japanese form it consists of a count of 17 syllables and is printed in a single vertical line. In *Short and Sweet: 101 Very Short Poems* edited by Simon Armitage there is a case made for the following being the world's briefest poem – although this shortest of the shorts does bear a title:

Fleas

Adam
'ad 'em

Consider this six-word story, attributed to Ernest Hemingway, "For sale. Baby shoes. Never worn." For me, it exemplifies brevity, giving a sense of the poetic compost in which my terset has gestated.

A POINT ABOUT PUNCTUATION

The creators of the Northern Poetry Library's branding realized the importance of the period, basing their design around the decimal point utilized in library systems: the stop divides numbers so books can be classified. In poetry, a full-stop is a grammatical heavyweight of prosody and white space: it is a pause, a breath, a time to reflect. The punctuation in my new form literally and aesthetically anchors the three words to the page: as a holdfast is to seaweed, so the full stop is to a terset, tethering it in the ocean of language with a poetical context, and giving it a kind of upended title. This gives space for play – and as soon as we shared the form people started extending and disrupting it with other grammatical marks, with longer lines and with spacing.

CAN A POEM REALLY BE JUST THREE WORDS AND A FULL STOP?

In the end I don't really know if an anchored terset is a poem. However, for me it's the question that is important – the question that is a motor to poetry's enduring appeal: *just what is a poem*? As TS Eliot said, "genuine poetry can communicate before it is understood." And how true too of life. What do we know of it other than we live it until our time is up? To leave a mark – however brief – feels important. Most societies and civilisations have valued poets and produced poetry in some form or another, signalling its significance in our lives. The Northern Poetry Library is hugely important in the advancement and preservation of the North East's poetic heritage: in the end *we* are that heritage, so in preserving it we celebrate and commemorate ourselves. The anchored tersets facing were contributed by library staff.

Novus
Poesis
Letificus

•

- Julie Brown

Now
Poetry
Lives

•

- Pat Hallam

Naturally
Polished
Limestone

•

- Chris Bennett

None
Poetry
Lover

•

- Shirley Appleby

Napoleon
Posing
Loftily

•

- Jo Currie

Northumbria's
Peaceful
Locations

•

- Joan Robson

Nonsense
Pretend
Language

•

- Kirsty White

Notorious
Piratical
Luminaries

•

- Jude Ozers

No
Puedo
Leer

•

- Deidre Cooper

Neatness
Pleases
Librarians

•

- Pat Hallam

About the poets-in-residence

Originally from the Midlands, DEGNA STONE is a poet and producer based in Tyne and Wear. She edits the online anthology Deseeded and is co-founder and Managing Editor of Butcher's Dog poetry magazine. Her poems have appeared in The Rialto, The Black Light Engine Room, Ink Sweat and Tears, and Diamond Twig, and she has published two poetry pamphlets, Between the Floorboards (ID on Tyne Press) and Record and Play (Red Squirrel Press). She received a Northern Writers' Award in 2015.

CAROLYN JESS-COOKE has an international profile as an author and academic. Her poetry has been published in New Statesman, Poetry Review, Poetry London and others, and has received an Eric Gregory Award, the Tyrone Guthrie Prize for Poetry, a place in the Cardiff International Poetry Competition, and has twice received a Northern Promise Award from New Writing North. Most recently, her poem Hare was commended in the National Poetry Competition and was made into a filmpoem. Carolyn's novels have been published in 23 languages and she is Lecturer in Creative Writing at the University of Glasgow.

JOHN CHALLIS, born in London, lives and works in the North East. He is a recipient of a Northern Writers' Award and a Pushcart Prize, and holds a PhD in Creative Writing from Newcastle University. His poetry has appeared in many journals and anthologies including Butcher's Dog, Clinic, Magma, Poetry London, The Rialto, and has been broadcast on BBC Radio 4. His debut play, The Next Train to Depart, premiered in Hexham in 2014. He is also a freelance teacher and workshop leader, and is an arts events producer.

JO COLLEY is a writer and artist interested in the presentation of creativity via the digital: film, audio, image, text. She writes poetry, makes poetry films and podcasts, and loves the sea and the countryside. She won the 2013 Read Our Lips Prize for Dream On, a poetry film. Her most recent poetry collection, Bones of Birds, was published by Smokestack in 2015. She is a visiting artist for the Year in Beadnell project.

LINDA FRANCE is based close to Hadrian's Wall, near Hexham, in Northumberland. Since 1992, she has published eight poetry collections with Bloodaxe, Smokestack and Arc; her latest is Reading the Flowers (Arc, 2016). She also edited the ground-breaking anthology Sixty Women Poets. Linda has worked on a number of collaborations with visual and sound artists and held a Leverhulme Residency at Newcastle University's Botanic Garden, Moorbank. She won First Prize in the 2013 National Poetry Competition and was Creative Writing Fellow at the University of Leeds 2015-16.

LISA MATTHEWS is a poet, writing researcher and collaborative artist based on the northeast coast of England. She has published a chapbook, 14, and three poetry collections, her most recent being The Eternally Packed Suitcase (Vane Women, 2015). She has a book of prose poems – working title Callisto – due out at the end of 2016, published by Red Squirrel Press. In spring 2016 she co-authored a poetic-visual essay Two Rivers & the Sea inspired by Rachel Carson and the Northumberland coast. You can view Lisa's work at http://lisamatthewswriter.dunked.com

Acknowledgements

With thanks to Wendy Scott, Cultural Development Manager at Active Northumberland for setting the Northern Poetry Project in motion and for her continued commitment and enthusiasm, and to Denise Alexander for whipping us into shape and ensuring participants and project parts are working together with reasonable harmony – no mean feat. And last, not least, to the often-unsung heroes/oines, the library staff at NPL and all the public libraries who have worked with us across our region.

This anthology, along with the activities and outputs from the Northern Poetry Library project, has been made possible through the support of Arts Council England, Active Northumberland and Northumberland County Council. Partners also include New Writing North, Palace Green Library, Durham University, Woodhorn Museum (Northumberland), the Scottish Poetry Library, Carcanet Press, Newcastle University and the Lit & Phil, Newcastle.